Amazing Habitats

OCEANS

W

FRANKLIN WATTS
LONDON • SYDNEY

This edition first published in 2015
by Franklin Watts
338 Euston Road
London NW1 3BH

Franklin Watts Australia
Level 17/207 Kent Street
Sydney, NSW 2000

A CIP catalogue record for this book
is available from the British Library.

ISBN: 978-1-4451-3204-4

Dewey no. 577.7

Printed in China

Franklin Watts is a division of
Hachette Children's Books,
an Hachette UK company.
www.hachette.co.uk

Note to parents and teachers concerning
websites: In the book every effort has been
made by the Publishers to ensure that
websites are suitable for children, that they
are of the highest educational value, and that
they contain no inappropriate or offensive
material. However, because of the nature of
the Internet, it is impossible to guarantee that
the contents of these sites will not be altered.
We advise that Internet access is supervised
by a responsible adult.

Author: Leon Gray
Designer: Karen Perry
Picture Researcher: Clare Newman
Editor: Tim Harris
Children's Publisher: Anne O'Daly
Design Manager: Keith Davis
Editorial Director: Lindsey Lowe

Picture Credits
The photographs in this book are used by
permission and through the courtesy of:

Front Cover, ©William Bradberry/Shutterstock:

1, ©Igor Zh/Shutterstock; 2-3, ©Neamov/
Shutterstock; 4b, ©Mogens Trolle/Shutterstock;
4-5, ©Brian Kinney/Shutterstock; 6tl, ©Tatiana
Ivkovich/Shutterstock; 6bl, ©Photoaeye/
Shutterstock; 7tr, ©Outdoorsman/Shutterstock;
7cr, ©Mogens Trolle/Shutterstock; 7bl, ©BMJ/
Shutterstock; 8-9, ©Bruno Ismael Silva Alves/
Shutterstock; 9, ©Studio Art/Shutterstock; 10-11,
©CB Pix/Shutterstock; 11tr, ©Photo Researchers/
FLPA; 12b, ©Distinctive Images/Shutterstock;
12-13, ©Alexander Sher/iStock/Thinkstock;
13br, ©Neonja/Richard Barte/Wikipedia; 14,
©Fomengto/Shutterstock; 15t, ©Ethan Daniels/
Shutterstock; 15b, ©Francis Abbott/Nature PL/
Alamy; 16, ©Isabelle Kvehn/Shutterstock; 16-17,
©Alterfalter/Shutterstock; 18-19, ©Igor Zh/
Shutterstock; 19tr, ©Laura D/Shutterstock; 20tr,
©John A. Anderson/Shutterstock; 20b, ©Andrea
Izzotti/Shutterstock; 21, ©Boris Pamikov/
Shutterstock; 22, ©Matt 9122/Shutterstock;
23t, ©Rich Carey/Shutterstock; 23b, ©Photo
Researchers/FLPA; 24, ©Nigel Pavitt/AWL Images/
Getty Images; 25t, ©Antoni Halim/Shutterstock;
25b, ©Trubavin/Shutterstock; 26-27, ©Tony
Moran/Shutterstock; 27t, ©Jeffrey Rotman/Corbis;
28cl, ©Mogens Trolle/Shutterstock; 28cr, ©Isabelle
Kvehn/Shutterstock; 28br, ©Ethan Daniels/
Shutterstock; 28-29, ©Brian Kinney/Shutterstock;
29cl, ©Trubavin/Shutterstock; 29bl, ©Jeffrey
Rotman/Corbis.

t=top, v=centre, b=bottom, l=left, r=right

Brown Bear Books Ltd has made every
attempt to contact the copyright holder.
If you have any information please contact
licensing@brownbearbooks.co.uk

CONTENTS

INTRODUCTION

Oceans cover more than two-thirds of our planet's surface. All oceans contain salty water. They are home to a huge variety of animals and plants.

Habitats are places where animals and plants live and grow. Some prefer dry deserts, while others live in tropical rainforests. The animals and plants that live in the world's oceans have **adapted** to live in salty water. Some animals and plants live near the surface of the water. Others are found far beneath the waves in the murky ocean depths.

Read on to find out what oceans are like – and how plants, animals and people live in and around them.

Grey whales live in the Pacific Ocean. They feed close to the ocean surface.

CORALS

Corals may look like plants, but they are animals. Corals live on the sea floor in warm, tropical water. Often, many corals grow together to form a coral reef. Many fish feed near the reefs.

OCEANS OF THE

This map shows the world's five oceans. The darker blue areas are the deepest parts of the oceans. The Pacific is the world's biggest ocean.

An orca, or killer whale, leaps from the water in the Pacific Ocean. This behaviour is called breaching.

A trawler returns to port after fishing for herring in the Atlantic Ocean off the coast of Canada.

NORTH AMERICA

ATLANTIC OCEAN

PACIFIC OCEAN

SOUTH AMERICA

SOUTHERN OCEAN

ANTARCTICA

WORLD

Ocean

Walruses rest on sea ice floating on the Arctic Ocean These **mammals** dive beneath the surface of the water to hunt fish.

ARCTIC OCEAN

EUROPE

ASIA

AFRICA

INDIAN OCEAN

AUSTRALIA

A great white shark hunts for squid in the Indian Ocean.

An emperor penguin jumps onto sea ice in the Southern Ocean.

CLIMATE AND

WATER WAVES

Wind blows over the surface of the ocean and creates waves. When very big waves crash onto the shore, spray blows inland.

The water that makes up the world's oceans is constantly on the move. It plays a big part in shaping Earth's weather. Oceans also have their own underwater zones, which change as you go deeper beneath the surface.

ZONES

Warm and cold water flow around the oceans in **currents**. The wind and the spinning movement of Earth in space combine to create these currents. A warm current called the Gulf Stream flows from tropical parts of the Atlantic Ocean. It reaches as far north as the coast of Britain. Wind that blows over the Gulf Stream also becomes warm. So does the land that the wind blows over. In this way, the temperature of the ocean changes the climate of the land nearby.

When there is litte or no wind, the surface of the ocean may seem flat and still, but currents keep the water on the move below.

Ocean zones

There are three main ocean zones between the surface of the water and the sea floor. The top zone is called the **sunlit zone** because it is bathed in sunlight during the day. Most ocean animals and plants live in the sunlit zone. As you sink deeper into the **twilight zone**, the light fades, the water gets cooler and the **water pressure** increases. The **dark zone** is at the bottom of the ocean depths. This is a world of total darkness. Few animals and no plants can survive in this extreme environment.

A blacktip reef shark swims near a shoal of small fish in the sunlit zone of the Indian Ocean.

DEEP FISH

In 2008 a **shoal** of 17 fish was found in a very deep part of the dark zone in the Pacific Ocean. Called *Pseudoliparis*, the fish were swimming 7,700 metres (25,270 feet) below the surface.

The hatchetfish lives in the dark zone of the world's oceans.

PLANTS

Most of the ocean's plant life consists of algae. Most algae drift in ocean currents and provide food for sea creatures. Other plants live in coastal regions, where the ocean meets the land.

Most algae that live in the ocean are tiny. They can only be seen under a **microscope**. Algae are not true plants. They do not have roots, stems and leaves like plants that grow on the land. Like true plants, algae need sunlight to grow. They can grow on the ocean shore and in the top 200 metres (660 feet) of the ocean. Light does not reach any deeper than that, so algae cannot grow there.

The seaweed that washes up on beaches is a type of algae. People collect seaweed to eat. The green or brown fronds look like the leaves of plants that grow on land.

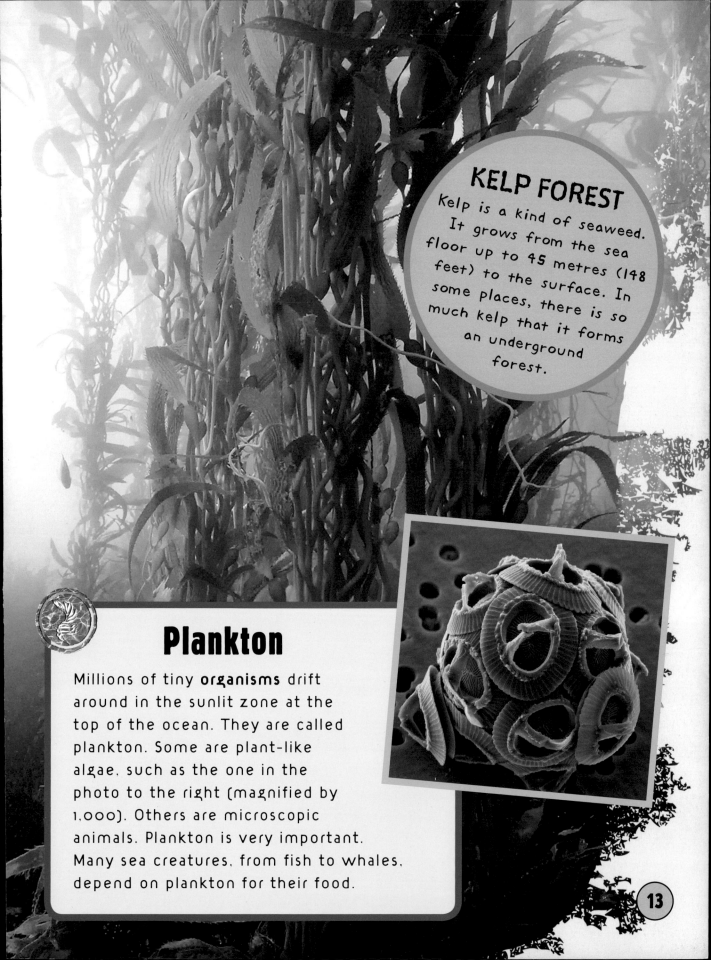

Plankton

Millions of tiny **organisms** drift around in the sunlit zone at the top of the ocean. They are called plankton. Some are plant-like algae, such as the one in the photo to the right (magnified by 1,000). Others are microscopic animals. Plankton is very important. Many sea creatures, from fish to whales, depend on plankton for their food.

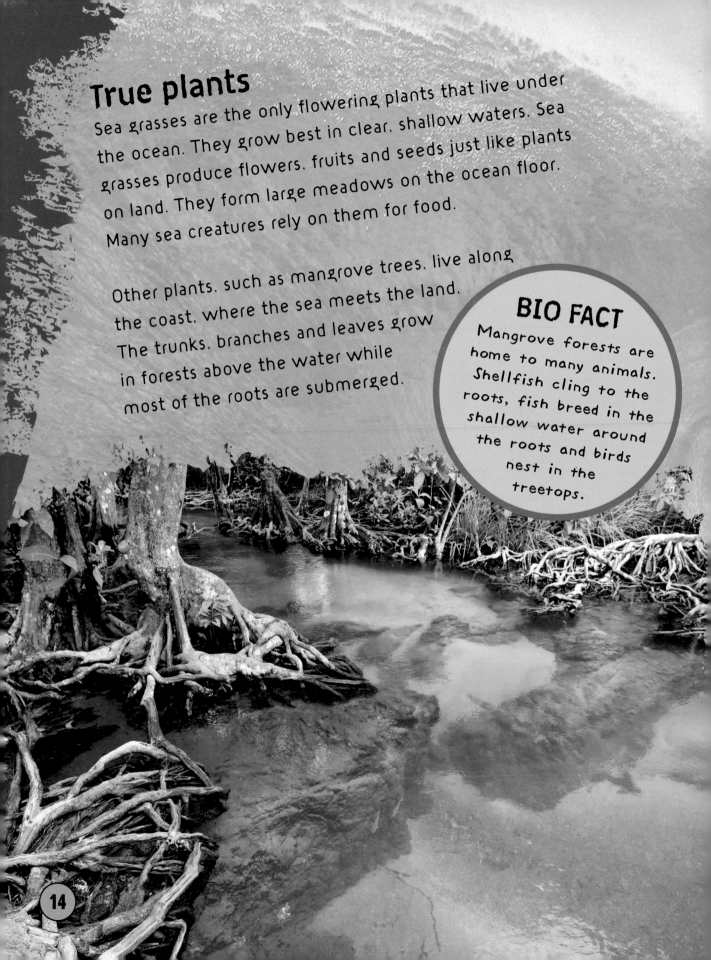

True plants

Sea grasses are the only flowering plants that live under the ocean. They grow best in clear, shallow waters. Sea grasses produce flowers, fruits and seeds just like plants on land. They form large meadows on the ocean floor. Many sea creatures rely on them for food.

Other plants, such as mangrove trees, live along the coast, where the sea meets the land. The trunks, branches and leaves grow in forests above the water while most of the roots are submerged.

BIO FACT
Mangrove forests are home to many animals. Shellfish cling to the roots, fish breed in the shallow water around the roots and birds nest in the treetops.

Trees on stilts

Mangrove trees look like they are growing on stilts. The 'stilts' are special roots that anchor the tree in the mud and prop it above the water. These roots filter out salt from the seawater. Mangrove trees store the salt in their leaves. After a while, the trees get rid of the excess salt by shedding some of their leaves.

Neptune grass grows on the ocean floor in the Mediterranean Sea. One colony near the Spanish island of Ibiza is more than 100,000 years old.

ANIMALS

You can find different animals in every part of the ocean, from the surface all the way down to the sea floor. Some animals spend all of their lives under the water. Others use the oceans to hunt or mate but live mostly on the land.

- Green sea turtles use their enormous flippers like paddles to swim quickly through the water.

Green sea turtle

Sea turtles live in the warm waters of the Atlantic, Pacific and Indian oceans. Male green sea turtles never leave the water. Females come ashore every two years to lay their eggs. These turtles can hold their breath for hours as they swim underwater looking for food. Young turtles eat crabs and jellyfish but adults are **vegetarians**.

In shallow waters, crabs and starfish roam across the sea floor. In some tropical waters, corals grow in huge reefs. These reefs provide shelter for other animals, such as anemones, eels, reef sharks and urchins. Further out to sea, large fish, turtles and whales swim in the open ocean in search of food. Some animals, such as anglerfish and tube worms, have even adapted to life in the murky ocean depths.

SHOAL OF FISH

In a single group, or shoal, of sardines, there may be thousands of fish. When the shoal changes direction every fish moves at exactly the same time.

Sea mammals

Sea mammals are similar to land mammals. They all have warm blood and breathe air into their lungs. But sea mammals are adapted to life in the water. They have a thick layer of fat to keep them warm in the cold seawater. They can hold their breath for some time underwater, but they also need to rise to the surface to breathe. Common sea mammals include dolphins, dugongs and seals.

FOOD CYCLE

In some places, cool ocean currents bring **nutrients** to the surface. Plankton feed on these nutrients. Fish eat the plankton. Dolphins and whales then eat the fish.

Dorsal fin

Flipper

Bottlenose dolphins leap out of the water as they swim through the open ocean. Bottlenose dolphins live in groups, or pods, with up to 30 members. They hunt fish, shrimp and squid in the top layer of the ocean.

Remora fish follow the dugong as it feeds

Beak is shaped like a bottle

Ocean herbivores

On the land, **herbivores** such as cattle, sheep, wildebeest and zebras, graze on grasslands. In the ocean, swimming herbivores called dugongs graze on sea grasses and algae on the ocean floor. For this reason, dugongs are sometimes called 'sea cows'. These sea mammals live in tropical parts of the Indian and Pacific oceans. They can hold their breath for up to six minutes while they feed.

19

Life on the ocean floor

In places where the ocean is shallow, the ocean floor may have coral reefs, mudflats, and rocky and sandy areas. But the ocean floor is usually much deeper, thousands of metres below the surface. Animals adapt to life in these places in different ways. Some, such as flatfish, live just under the sea bed. Others, such as anemones, attach themselves to coral reefs. Deep-sea animals, such as tube worms, live in total darkness and under extreme pressure.

FISH FOOD

Copepods are some of the most common animals in the world. These tiny animals look like mini shrimps. If copepods did not exist, many fish in the ocean would go hungry!

A giant octopus uses its tentacles to feel its way across the sea bed. This octopus eats fish, including small sharks.

Colourful hunter

Some animals creep along the ocean floor in search of food. They include colourful **predators** called sea slugs. They eat other animals, including other sea slugs! Some have **toxins** in their bodies that harm any animal that eats them. A sea slug's bright colours warn other animals that it is dangerous to eat them.

Giant clams float in the water when they are young. When they become adults they settle on the sea bed and stay there.

Top predators

The ocean's top predators sit at the very top of the **food chain**. They are animals that no other animals hunt for food. Top ocean predators include fearsome fish, such as sharks and also sea mammals, such as blue whales – the world's biggest animal. Perhaps the deadliest of all sea predators is the killer whale. These intelligent animals hunt in packs. Killer whales will eat almost anything they can catch, from fish and squid to seals, sea lions and other whales. They have even been known to attack great white sharks!

Dorsal fin helps shark change direction

Eye

A hammerhead shark's eyes are at the end of stalks that stick out on either side of its head. The shark can see above and below itself at all times.

Mouth

Eye can see up and down

REEF HUNTER

Reef sharks swim near coral reefs and hunt fish and squid. These sharks are agile swimmers. They can twist and turn at great speed.

Deep predators

Fangfish live in the murky ocean depths, 2,800 metres (9,200 feet) beneath the surface. Light cannot reach this far so fangfish live in the dark. However, these fish can make their own light, called **bioluminescence**. The fangfish switch off this body light when they are hunting so that their prey cannot see them.

23

PEOPLE

People have a strong bond with the oceans. The water provides a source of food, including seaweed, fish and shellfish. People use ships to carry themselves and their goods across the world.

FISH FOOD

A fisherman waits to spear a fish in the shallow waters of Lake Turkana, Kenya. This is an ancient method of fishing.

People have always relied on the oceans for survival. Traditional fishing techniques use spears, small nets or rods to catch fish. For some, this is still the only way they can feed their families. Today, fishing is also a huge industry. In fact, so many fish are caught in fishing nets that some, such as cod, are in danger of being wiped out. Before trains, cars and planes were invented, the oceans were the best way for people to travel around the world. They first used simple wooden rafts, then sailing ships. Modern cargo ships are powered by engines and carry food, clothes and other goods from country to country.

Huge ships called supertankers carry oil thousands of miles across the world's oceans.

Ocean fun

Today, one of the most popular uses of the ocean is for water sports, such as diving, sailing, swimming and surfing. Every year, many families go to beach resorts for their holidays. There they can relax together and enjoy these leisure pursuits.

THE FUTURE

The world's oceans are a valuable resource. People have to work together to protect them from harmful pollution and overfishing.

In the last 100 years, the oceans have come under serious threat. People have taken large amounts of valuable resources from the sea, such as fish and oil. Human activities have also created problems, such as pollution, **climate change** and **global warming**.

WIND FARMS

Most electricity we use comes from burning fossil fuels. This creates pollution. Wind farms are a cleaner way to generate electricity. They use the energy of the wind instead.

Scientists explore the ocean depths in submersibles. They study the oceans in order to help protect them.

Rising sea levels

If Earth's temperature continues to rise due to global warming, polar ice will melt. Sea levels will rise and many islands will disappear. At the same time, pollution is destroying ocean habitats such as coral reefs. Many sea creatures are dying out. Countries around the world now recognise these problems. They are working together to protect the oceans so future generations of people can enjoy them.

QUIZ

Try this quiz to test your knowledge of ocean habitats. You can find the answers on page 31.

1 This is a grey whale. Which of the world's oceans does it live in?

2 Green sea turtles spend almost all their lives at sea. Why do females sometimes come ashore?

3 What type of seaweed can be found growing in huge forests from the ocean floor?

Fact File

- The world's oceans cover more than two-thirds of Earth's surface area.

- There are five main oceans – the Pacific, Atlantic, Indian, Arctic and Southern oceans.

- The three main ocean zones are called the sunlit, twilight and dark zones.

- The most common plant life in the ocean are plant-like algae, such as seaweed.

4 Can you name three other popular water sports apart from surfing?

5 This vehicle is used to explore the ocean depths. What is it called?

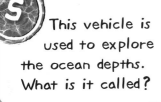

Winners and losers

⬆ Some gulls have learned to feed on rubbish dumps. They have more food to give their chicks and can raise larger families.

⬇ Hammerhead sharks could die out because so many are being fished for food.

⬇ The number of sea turtles in the oceans is falling. People hunt them and eat their eggs. Many turtles are also caught in fishing nets.

GLOSSARY

adapted: When an animal or plant has slowly changed to fit in with its surroundings.

bioluminescence: The process of producing light from inside the bodies of living things. Some deep-sea fish use bioluminescence to trap prey and send signals to other deep-sea fish.

climate change: The warming of Earth's climate produced by the increase in greenhouse gases in the atmosphere.

currents: The movement of cool and warm water beneath the surface of the ocean.

dark zone: The zone at the very bottom of the ocean. The dark zone is in complete darkness.

food chain: The order in which animals feed on plants and other animals within a habitat.

global warming: The gradual increase in Earth's temperature caused by human activities, such as burning fossil fuels.

habitats: The places where animals and plants live together.

herbivores: Animals that eat only plants. Sea mammals called dugongs are herbivores, as are land mammals such as sheep and zebras.

mammals: Animals with warm blood that breathe air using lungs. Mammals feed their young on milk.

microscope: An instrument that is used to see extremely small objects.

nutrients: something in food that helps living things live and grow.

organisms: A scientific word to describe any living thing, such as an animal or plant.

predators: Animals that hunt and eat other animals.

shoal: A large group of fish.

sunlit zone: The zone at the very top of the ocean. The sunlit zone is bathed in sunlight during the day.

toxins: Any substances produced by animals and plants that can harm other living things.

twilight zone: An ocean zone that lies between the sunlit zone and the dark zone. As you move deeper down the twilight zone, the light fades, the water gets colder and the water pressure increases.

vegetarians: Animals that do not eat the bodies of other animals.

water pressure: The weight of water that pushes down on things in the ocean.

FURTHER RESOURCES

Books

Calver, Paul and Reynolds, Toby. *Visual Explorers: Ocean Life.* Franklin Watts (2014).

Hewitt, Sally. *Project Geography: The Sea.* Franklin Watts (2012).

Levete, Sarah. *Protecting Our Planet: Destroying the Oceans.* Wayland (2012).

Royston, Angela. *Research On the Edge: Oceans.* Wayland (2014).

Websites

NASA's Climate Kids. The American space agency's 'Eyes on the Earth' website includes lots of information on oceans and what we can do to protect them.
http://climatekids.nasa.gov/menu/ocean/

National Geographic site on oceans. Learn all about the world's oceans and the amazing animals and plants that live in them. Includes stunning photographs and videos, and material on climate change.
oceans.nationalgeographic.com/ocean/ocean-life/

Natural History Museum. Find out about the many different animals that live in the world's oceans. You will meet some surprising sharks, a giant squid, a stranded whale and a mimic octopus.
www.nhm.ac.uk/kids-only/life/life-sea/index.html

World Wide Fund for Nature. Photos, videos, ocean animals and plants, and conservation plans for the world's ocean habitats.
www.worldwildlife.org/habitats/oceans

Answers to the Quiz: **1** Pacific Ocean. **2** To lay their eggs. **3** Kelp. **4** Diving, sailing and swimming. **5** A submersible.

INDEX